ISBN 978-1-330-11596-1
PIBN 10029629

1 MONTH OF
FREE
READING

at
www.ForgottenBooks.com

By purchasing this book you are eligible for one month membership to ForgottenBooks.com, giving you unlimited access to our entire collection of over 1,000,000 titles via our web site and mobile apps.

To claim your free month visit:

www.forgottenbooks.com/free29629

English
Français
Deutsche
Italiano
Español
Português

www.forgottenbooks.com

Mythology Photography **Fiction**
Fishing Christianity **Art** Cooking
Essays Buddhism Freemasonry
Medicine **Biology** Music **Ancient
Egypt** Evolution Carpentry Physics
Dance Geology **Mathematics** Fitness
Shakespeare **Folklore** Yoga Marketing
Confidence Immortality Biographies
Poetry **Psychology** Witchcraft
Electronics Chemistry History **Law**
Accounting **Philosophy** Anthropology
Alchemy Drama Quantum Mechanics
Atheism Sexual Health **Ancient History**
Entrepreneurship Languages Sport
Paleontology Needlework Islam
Metaphysics Investment Archaeology
Parenting Statistics Criminology
Motivational

FIFTY YEARS OF
AMERICAN EDUCATION

A SKETCH OF THE PROGRESS
OF EDUCATION IN THE UNITED STATES
FROM 1867 TO 1917

BY

ERNEST CARROLL MOORE

GINN AND COMPANY

BOSTON · NEW YORK · CHICAGO · LONDON
ATLANTA · DALLAS · COLUMBUS · SAN FRANCISCO

JAN -8 1918

The Athenæum Press

GINN AND COMPANY · PRO-
PRIETORS · BOSTON · U S.A.

©CI.A479920

1867–1917

IN THE year *1867* Edwin Ginn took desk room in a modest Boston office and so began the business which has for many years been conducted under the firm name of Ginn and Company. When an individual or an organization reaches the half-century mark it seems fitting to signalize in some appropriate way that achievement. Casting about for a suitable anniversary memento of our own fifty years, we were struck by the remarkable growth and development of the school system of the United States during this period.

It finally seemed to us that we could do no better than invite Dr. Ernest C. Moore to sum up the educational progress of the United States since *1867*. We are sure that Dr. Moore's admirable sketch of the history of education in this country for the period beginning in *1867* and ending in *1917* will be a welcome and useful contribution to our educational literature, and we bring it before the public with gratitude that our own business development has been contemporaneous with this marvelous change in our American schools.

GINN AND COMPANY

November, 1917

CONTENTS

FIFTY YEARS OF
AMERICAN EDUCATION

CHAPTER I

OTHING seems more certain than *We live* that this is a dynamic universe, in *in a* which all things change, for activity *Period of* *Change* is their law. Yet the changes which everywhere go on take place so imperceptibly that it is only when their effects are massed that we begin to note their existence. Something very like a torrent of change has been pushing life forward in the United States since the Civil War, and we who are caught up in its onrushing have been carried along too swiftly to be aware of the distance we have traveled or the speed at which we are moving. Francis Galton declared that man's work in clearing the forests of North America " would be visible to an observer as far off as the moon," yet we who dwell in the land that that clearing made habitable tend to think of its physical features as always having been the same as they now are. That same statifying tendency benumbs our perception

3

throughout. I heard President Eliot say in a recent address that the last fifty years has been "the most prodigious period of change through which the world has ever passed." Most of us do not think of it in that way.

Let us note a few of the changes which came on the heels of the Civil War. The first transatlantic cable was laid in 1866. The first transcontinental railway was operated in 1869. Bell's first telephone bears the date 1875, and telephone exchanges were instituted in 1879. The first cable car line was started in San Francisco in 1873. Electric lighting dates from 1876 and electric traction from 1880. The Mergenthaler linotype was completed in 1884. In 1885 Daimler invented the internal combustion motor, and in 1894 the first trial run of automobiles was organized by a French newspaper. In 1896 Marconi produced an operative electric-wave telegraph. Langley tested his steam-driven flying machine in 1893, and in 1903 the Wright brothers made their first flight in a motor-driven aëroplane. In 1877 Holland constructed his first submarine. The first dreadnought made its trial run in 1906. *We live* New guns, of long range, accuracy, and rapidity *in a* of fire, and high explosives contributed an in- *Period of Change* strument of slaughter which the combined power of mankind is hardly able to keep from destroying the human race. If tools are but the elongation of the human hand, man's arm has been mightily lengthened during the last half century.

But progress in mechanical inventions is but one phase of the development of science. Perhaps the most significant changes of all have taken place in medicine. " Forty years ago," says Sir William Osler, "the world did not know the cause of any of the great infections. . . . Of all the great camp diseases — plague, cholera, malaria, yellow fever, typhoid fever, typhus, and dysentery — we know the mode of transmission, and of all but yellow fever, the germs. Man has now control of the most malign of Nature's forces in a way never dreamt of by our fathers. . . . Half a century has done more than a hundred centuries to solve the problem of the first importance in his progress."

Such are a few of the revolutionary changes which science has ushered in in the brief period of the half century which will, it seems, be known in history as the scientific age. Darwin's epochal discovery had been given to the world in 1859. Huxley, Spencer, Pasteur, Berthelot, Joule, Clerk Maxwell, Tait, and Kelvin were at work and Faraday was still alive when the period we are studying began. The creation of the sciences, always a slow process, had reached a period of intensification.

Science is an active force which infiltrates all human relations. The discovery which Darwin made has wrought no less significant changes in religious, moral, political, social, and philosophical conceptions than have steam and electricity in the way of mechanical assistance. In view of its enlarged comprehension and the changed attitudes which that enlarged comprehension entails, it is nothing short of exact truth to say that in the last half century the race has achieved a new heaven and a new earth.

If we ask how it has been with our country during this period we shall find that immense

6

social transformations have taken place. First *We live* came the ever-to-be regretted period of recon- *in a* struction and at the same time the rapid de- *Period of* velopment of the farming regions of the great *Change* West. Then in rapid succession came civil-service reform, great labor agitations, the Sherman Antitrust Act, the panic of 1893, and the widespread agitation for monetary legislation which it caused. Then came the war with Spain, in which the United States took possession of Cuba and restored that island to its rightful owners, drove Spain from the Philippine Islands and determined to retain them until such time as they might safely be intrusted to their own inhabitants, thus forsaking its previous policy of isolation to become an active member of the family of the great powers of the world. The Pacific was joined to the Atlantic, the franchise was extended to women in several states, immigrants poured into the country by the million. The desert was reclaimed; farm acreage was extended by an area that exceeded the territory of the German Empire. Industrialism grew, cities doubled and trebled their populations, great combinations of skilled and unskilled workers were formed. Political radicalism gained control and semisocialistic programs of reform were enacted into laws.

Have changes at all comparable with these taken place in education? Has the progress of invention, the advance of science, the onrushing development of social, economic, and political life been accompanied by a corresponding development in the schools of the nation? Progress in education follows progress in other activities of life. It is apt to follow somewhat afar off, for the school is a conserving rather than a renewing force. The battle of ideas does not rage in it as it rages in the world. Its first duty is to teach, and before it can do so confidently it must be assured of the validity and the great worth of what it teaches. Adults are far more ready to try experiments upon themselves than upon their children. The young, they feel, must not be endangered by innovations. Only that which has been tested and proved, although usually by time rather than by merit, has a claim upon their attention. The school, therefore, sits somewhat

8

apart from the current of change. Yet there is *We live* a relation between educational advance and in- *in a* dustrial and civic progress, and in a democracy *Period of* *Change* it must, in a measure, overcome its tendency to aloofness and make itself the responsive servant of the public need. This it has done and is doing, and, as a consequence, the changes which have taken place in education in the last fifty years are momentous.

CHAPTER II

TO PROVIDE a background for our
picture let us take note of the significant educational movements which
had been set afoot before the period which we
are to study began, in order that we may know
its historical heredity. In Massachusetts localism
obtained its greatest control over education in
the decentralized district school about the year
1827. There were only two functions which the
districts could not perform. One was the levying
and apportioning of taxes and the other was the
certificating of teachers, both of these functions
being retained by the towns. The school district
is the minutest subdivision into which govern-
mental authority has ever been broken, and under
its control of instruction public education de-
clined to its nadir. The process by which the
school districts thus unhappily opposed the general welfare and obtained a destructive measure
of local control was at least a century long. It

brought about the undoing of the town grammar schools and provided only very inferior
neighborhood schools in place of them. In self-
defense the wealthier folks here and there established private academies to obtain a better
education for their children, and in time the
state aided them with grants of public money.
These schools were free in the sense that they
were open to all who could meet their conditions, but their tuition fees had to be paid.

But about the year 1800 an immense change
had begun to come over the land. The invention
of the steam engine had started a mighty
transformation in the life of the people. Do-
mestic industry was supplanted by the factory
system. The factories which sprang up needed
workers, and people flocked from the country
into the towns. At first the towns were little
better than hastily constructed camps without
adequate housing, adequate sanitation, adequate
police and health regulations. Ignorance, dis-
ease, drunkenness, poverty, and crime flourished
in them. Then came the hard times of 1819–
1821, which made conditions so desperate that

great humanitarian movements took form to alleviate them. Among these were the temperance movement; the labor movement; the philanthropic movement to care for the poor, to provide hospitals for the insane, to combat the increase of crime and furnish training to the deaf, dumb, and blind; and, most important of all, a mighty movement in behalf of popular education, preaching a veritable crusade against the evils of the time by the creation of tax-supported public schools. This is the period of our educational revival which after-years may look back upon as no less significant in human history than the Renaissance or the Reformation.

The names of the humanitarians are on the honor roll of the nation. Among them are the educational revivalists. James G. Carter is their leader and more than any other is responsible for starting the great school reform. He fought valiantly against the two causes which seemed to him to be chiefly responsible for the failure of free schools: bad teachers and poor books. The state, he said, must go into the business of training teachers, and must provide that training

13

without cost to them. He outlined an institution which would do this, and declared that only by its creation could standards of qualification be set, and stability, dignity, and power be given to the teaching profession. He did not succeed immediately in persuading the state of Massachusetts to authorize the founding of normal schools, but he was the prime mover in that enterprise and one of the founders of that oldest of teachers' associations, the American Institute of Instruction, which took form in 1829. That organization met in Boston. Its membership was composed largely of teachers and educational leaders from New England; but representatives from the Middle, the Southern, and the Western states were present at its meetings and gave the society a national character from its very beginning. Its purpose was "to do something toward elevating the standard and increasing the efficiency of popular instruction," says the preface to the first volume of its Proceedings. "It will furnish the means, by the coöperation of its members, of obtaining an exact knowledge of the present condition of the

14

schools in all parts of the country. It will tend to render universal, so that it shall pervade every district and village, a strong conviction of the paramount national importance of preserving and extending the means of popular instruction, thus securing the aid of multitudes of fellow laborers in every portion of the country. It will tend to raise the standard of the qualification of instructors, so that the business of teaching shall not be the last resort of dullness and indolence, but shall be considered, as it was in the days of republican Greece, an occupation worthy of the highest talents and ambition. It will hardly fail to show that education is a science, to be advanced, like every other science, by experiment; whose principles are to be fixed and capacities determined by experiment; which is to be entered upon by men of a philosophical mind and pursued with a philosophical spirit. It will be likely to bring forward the modes and objects of instruction in foreign nations and ancient times and their applicability to the state of things among ourselves."[1]

[1] From the preface to the first volume of the Proceedings of The American Institute of Instruction.

The nation now had a parliament for "the diffusion of useful knowledge in regard to education." The cry had been sounded that "this country ought to be the best educated on the face of the earth," and its educational leaders were now organized to make it so.

Other revivalists of education were Samuel R. Hall, who founded at Andover in the year 1829 a seminary for teachers, a private normal school and the first real school for teachers in the United States; Horace Mann, the protagonist of public education, who having worked with the others of that splendid company to create the first State Board of Education in Massachusetts, in 1837 became its secretary; Charles Brooks, who without compensation traveled over New England, preaching the gospel of free public education; George B. Emerson, the prime mover in forming the Boston Mechanics' Institution in 1827; and Henry Barnard, "the Educator." They preached the doctrine that universal education is necessary to increase production, to diminish crime, to prevent poverty, to preserve free institutions, and to prevent the creation of a caste system, and that it is one of the natural rights of man. The people heard them gladly. The pioneers in the West and the laboring men in the cities lent valiant support to the cause.

Of Horace Mann and his work something more must be said even in so brief an account as this is intended to be. In 1836 the directors of the American Institute of Instruction presented a memorial to the legislature of Massachusetts, "showing the inefficiency of the means now employed for the education of the teachers of the common schools and praying the legislature to do something for their better instruction." They asked it to appoint a superintendent of the common schools. Governor Everett, however, in his message to the legislature recommended the creation of a state board of education; and, very fortunately for the future of the public schools of the nation, since no lone and unsupported superintendent could have done what was required unaided, the governor's recommendation prevailed. Accordingly, in 1837, a State Board of Education, made up of the governor and lieutenant-governor as ex-officio members and of eight others appointed by the governor, came into being. The Board was authorized to appoint a secretary whose duty was to be "to collect information of the actual conditions and efficiency of the common schools and other means of popular education and to diffuse as widely as possible throughout every part of the commonwealth information of the most approved and successful modes of instruction."

Mr. Horace Mann, an attorney-at-law of Dedham, who was the presiding officer of the senate of Massachusetts, championed the bill from the first. His keen interest in the cause of education, his activity in many lines of public reform, and his readiness to work without sparing himself led the governor to appoint him as one of the members of the new Board. "For myself," he writes, "I never had a sleeping or waking dream that I should ever think of myself or be thought of by any other in relation to" the post of secretary. Twenty days before the appointment of the new Board was announced such a suggestion was made to him by one who was in the confidence of the governor and was, like himself, to be a member of the Board. Was Mr. Mann fitted for such a post? He had not been professionally trained for educational leadership, but nobody else had been then. He had not served the cause of public education as had Mr. James G. Carter, who for years had urged school reform in Massachusetts. But he had served the people most acceptably in a position of leadership. He was a trained and successful lawyer, a man of great talent, and no one alive was more interested than he in the welfare of humanity or more eager to serve its helplessness and need. Indeed, he was a kind of knight-errant of the holy spirit, laborious and self-denying to a fault, one of the finest and most useful of all the great men whom our country has yet produced. "By their fruits ye shall know them." Judged in the light of what he did for public-school education in America, the members of the Board of Education seem to have been inspired in their choice of their secretary.

The words of the fathers are both interesting and profitable. How did this first *de facto*

19

superintendent of schools in our country regard his work? Of the Board of Education he writes:

It is the first great movement toward an organized system of common education which shall be at once thorough and universal. Every civilized state is imperfectly organized without a minister or secretary of instruction, as it would be without ministers or secretaries of state, finance, war, or the navy. Every child should be educated; if not educated by its own father, the state should appoint a father to it. I would much sooner surrender a portion of the territory of the commonwealth to an ambitious neighbor than I would surrender the minds of its children to the dominion of ignorance. . . . When will society, like a mother, take care of all her children?

When he is pressed for an answer whether he will accept the secretaryship of the Board, he writes in his diary:

I cannot think of that station as regards myself without feeling both hopes and fears, desires and apprehensions multiplying in my mind—so glorious a sphere should it be crowned with success, so heavy a disappointment and humiliation should it fail through any avoidable misfortune. What a thought, to have the future minds of such multitudes dependent in any perceptible degree upon one's own exertions! It is such a thought as must mightily energize or totally overpower any mind that can adequately comprehend it.

And when on the 29th of June, 1837, this first American director of the education of the young is elected to his high responsibility, we find him writing down a prayer for "an annihilation of selfishness, a mind of wisdom, a heart of benevolence" and resolving within himself, as both he and all his sons of the office have such good need to, that there is but one spirit in which the impediments raised by men of one motive, who are incased in jealousy and prejudice and intent only upon gain for themselves, can be met, and that is the spirit of self-abandonment—the spirit of the martyr.

I must not irritate, I must not humble, I must not degrade anyone in his own eyes. I must not present myself as a solid body to oppose, an iron barrier to any. I must be a fluid sort of man, adapting myself to tastes, opinions, habits, manners, so far as this can be done without hypocrisy or insincerity or a compromise of principle. In all this there must be a higher principle than to win personal esteem, or favor, or worldly applause. A new fountain may now be opened.

21

Let me strive to direct its current in such a manner that if when I have departed from life I may still be permitted to witness its course, I may behold it broadening and deepening in an everlasting progression of virtue and happiness. . . . I have faith in the improvability of men—in their accelerating improvability.

Such was his consecration and such was his creed.

By 1850 the New England doctrine of tax-supported free schools had been accepted in all the Northern States, and free schools had made their appearance in some of the states of the South. The normal school was from the first an essential feature, perhaps the chief feature of this great democratic movement for popular education. In 1839–1840 Massachusetts created three of them, at Lexington, Barre, and Bridgewater. Other states soon established them. It followed that if the schools were to be of the people, for the people, and by the people, the endowed academies must be superseded by public high schools. The first high school had been established by the municipality of Boston in 1821. Neighboring towns soon created

22

similar ones. Philadelphia in 1838 established
the Central High School; Baltimore opened
a city college and Providence created a high
school in 1843; and Hartford made over her
grammar school into a high school in 1847.

It was fortunate for the nation that the claims
of education were so incomparably championed
at the time when the life of the states was beginning to take organized form. But for what the
educational revivalists did and stimulated others
to do in other parts of the land, the nation might
have been very different from what it has been
and will be, and education might have had but
a small and insignificant part in it. As it was,
the foundations which they put down had only
been laid, when the question of slavery and the
all-absorbing Civil War claimed the attention
of men, and what they had so finely begun had
to be taken up as unfinished business and carried
to completion when the war was over and life
had once more resumed its proper course.

The year 1867 witnessed that great resump-
tion of the nation's proper business. On March 2
of that year an act establishing a department

of education was approved, the first section of which reads as follows:

Be it enacted by the Senate and the House of Representatives of the United States of America, in Congress assembled, that there shall be established at the city of Washington, a Department of Education for the purpose of collecting such statistics and facts as shall show the condition and progress of education in the several States and Territories, and of diffusing such information respecting the organization and management of school systems and methods of teaching as shall aid the people of the United States in the establishment and maintenance of efficient school systems and otherwise promote the cause of education throughout the country.

That tireless struggler for public schools, Henry Barnard, was appointed the first Commissioner of Education, and at the end of one year in office, on March 15, 1868, he submitted his first report. That report contains priceless material concerning the history of education in our country, not the least of which is the speech made by James A. Garfield of Ohio in support of the bill to establish a national bureau of education which a select committee, of which he was chairman, had reported to the House on the memorial of the National Association of School Superintendents.

There were 36 states in the United States at that time. Even the Congressional Library contained no educational reports whatever from 19 of them. The other 17 had raised by taxation $34,000,000 annually for the support and maintenance of public schools during the five years of war. The Census of 1860 showed that there were in the United States 115,224 common schools, 150,241 teachers, and 5,477,037 scholars. According to the same census there were 1,218,311 free white inhabitants of the United States over twenty-one years of age who could not read or write, and 871,418 of these were American-born citizens. Their number had been growing alarmingly. Mr. Mann added 30 per cent to these figures for "undoubted underestimates," and some persons went so far as to declare that one fourth of the population were illiterate. A third of a million immigrants were arriving every year, a large proportion of whom were uneducated, and 4,000,000 slaves had just been admitted to citizenship by the events of the war. "Such, Sir," said Mr. Garfield, "is the immense force which we must now confront by the genius of our institutions and the light of our civilization. How shall it be done? An American citizen can give but one answer. We must pour upon them the light of our public schools. We must make them intelligent, industrious, patriotic citizens, or they will drag us and our children down to their level."

The work to be done in the new era which began at the close of the Civil War was gigantic, but the American spirit had been re-created and balked at nothing. What were the agencies already in existence which it could employ in the resolute fight for internal development to which it now gave itself? Public education was now definitely regarded as a national interest. It is not only the birthright of the child but the state's indispensable means of self-preservation and improvement. Twenty-six states had by the beginning of the year 1867 created state school systems and state superintendents of public instruction to direct them. By that date there were 4 state normal schools in Massachusetts,

2 in New York, 1 in Michigan, 1 in New Jersey, 1 in Illinois, 4 in Pennsylvania, 5 in Wisconsin, 1 in Minnesota, 1 in California, 1 in
Indiana, 1 in South Carolina, 3 in Vermont, 1
in Kansas, 2 in Maine, 1 in Maryland, and 1
in Delaware. City normal schools had been
opened at New Haven, St. Louis, San Francisco,
and in 3 towns in Indiana and 3 in Iowa. Upon
the refusal of the legislature of Ohio to establish
such a school the State Teachers' Association
in 1855 started one. The report of the Commissioner of Education for the year 1870, a
precious volume because it contains the first
available body of statistics concerning the schools
of the United States, reports that in this year
no less than 369 colleges were in existence. In
1862, in the midst of the Civil War, Congress
had passed a bill granting to each state 30,000
acres of land for each senator and representative
in Congress. The income from the sale of this
land was, according to the directions of the bill,
to constitute a perpetual fund, and the interest
on that fund was to be used for "the endow-
ment, support, and maintenance of at least one

college" in which "the leading object should be, without excluding other scientific and classical studies, and including military tactics, to teach such branches of learning as are related to agriculture and the mechanic arts, in such manner as the Legislatures of the States may respectively prescribe, in order to promote the liberal and practical education of the industrial classes, in their several pursuits and professions in life." Nineteen states had established colleges before the end of 1861, the University of Pennsylvania having been created in 1755, the University of Vermont in 1791, the University of Virginia in 1825, the University of Indiana in 1828, the University of Michigan in 1837, and the University of Wisconsin in 1848.

If we turn now to the report of the Commissioner of Education for the year 1870, in order to learn where the educational battle was pitched, we shall find some interesting facts concerning the condition of education in the several states at that time.

The first free public school was established in California in 1849. In 1869 there were

28

73,754 children enrolled in 1268 schools. In the 1916 Report of the Commissioner of Education the whole number of pupils in school in that state is reported as 513,002.

Though the laws of the state of Connecticut laid an obligation upon every parent and guardian of children "not to suffer so much barbarism in any of their families as to have a single child or apprentice unable to read" and also "to bring them up to some lawful calling or employment," the rate bill existed in that state until the year 1868, when a law was passed requiring each town to "raise by taxation such sum of money as it may find necessary to make its schools free." The first year's trial of this measure demonstrated that some 6000 children had been kept from school by the rate bill. New Haven reports that it has maintained a system of graded schools for sixteen years.

Delaware replies to the request of the commissioner for information about its schools that it "is unable to supply reports asked for." There appears to have been a complete absence of supervision there.

The number of children attending school in the state of Illinois in 1868 was 706,780. The latest figure is 1,246,827. Only about 5 per cent of its schools were graded in 1867. "This small proportion of graded schools," writes the superintendent, "furnishes an impressive practical argument in favor of the abolition of the independent local school district. But while the adoption of the township system would remove all organic obstacles to the general prevalence of graded schools, it would not remove the misapprehension, prejudice, and indifference which so largely obtain in respect to the improved kinds of schools and methods of instruction." In this wise observation made fifty years ago, the need for the consolidation of schools is clearly stated and the obstacle which to this day has prevented that much agitated reform is pointed out.

The Superintendent of Schools of Indiana reports that although the constitution of the state makes it incumbent upon the legislature to provide "a general and uniform system of common schools wherein tuition shall be without charge and equally open to all, we cannot avoid the grave consideration that there is a large colored population in the state who have hitherto submitted patiently to the ordeal of adverse public sentiment and the force of our statutes in being denied participation in our public-school funds, while at the same time no bar can be discovered to their natural and constitutional right to these. . . . Colored citizens while hitherto deprived of their natural and constitutional rights have been subject to the special school tax for township purposes in common with white citizens, and have thus paid their proportion of expense for building schoolhouses for white children. After being denied all privilege to the school funds and thus taxed, they have been under the necessity of levying upon themselves an additional tax to build their own schoolhouses and for the entire cost of their tuition." This passage shows that since that day the people of the United States have, in at least one respect, grown considerably in grace and in justice.

Iowa reports that every civil township is a

school district and is divided into subdistricts
with subdirectors, each subdirector having
charge of the school affairs in his district.

It is a notable fact that persons are often chosen
for these positions without any reference to financial
ability or even common prudence. Much attention
is attached to the training in music which is given
in many of the graded schools. The old practice of
rote singing is discarded.

Kansas reports that though "the constitution
of the state provides that 'the 500,000 acres of
land granted to the new states under an act of
Congress distributing the proceeds of public
lands among the several states of the Union,
approved September 4, A. D. 1841, shall be in-
violably appropriated to the support of the
common schools,' notwithstanding this provision, the legislature of 1866 appropriated the
whole 500,000 acres to four railway companies."

The report of the Superintendent of Schools
of Kentucky gives an account of the struggle
of that state to obtain a reform in its school
laws which failed "through the ignorance and
prejudice of the legislature, notwithstanding a

previous decision of the people, by a majority of 20,000 votes, in favor of such reform. The common sentiment expressed was, 'Give us better laws and more money or abolish the school system altogether.' "

Michigan reports that " the plan of free schools has been in operation less than a single term, the legislature having only at the last session abolished the rate bill. In consequence of the schools being free, the length of time they have been held has been greatly increased. In some districts they are said to have nearly twice the length of school that they have previously had. The advantages of the free-school system are so manifest that it was adopted in most of the cities and large towns several years since, the rate being abolished by public vote. It is estimated that tuition in the graded schools is at least ten cents a month cheaper than in the schools which are not graded."

A New Hampshire superintendent, even in that early day, finds courage to protest against the study of grammar. "How vague and unsatisfactory the ideas which our pupils gain

33

from such terms as auxiliary, antecedent, correl- ative, coördinate, proposition, passive, imper- sonal, infinitive, logical, synopsis, etc." " But music," he writes, " is now a regular exercise, the same as arithmetic or geography."

The superintendent reports that in New Jersey there are 696 districts in which the schools are free and 634 in which they are sup- ported in part by tuition fees which the pupils pay. "If the action necessary to make schools free is not taken by the legislature soon, I am confident the people themselves will make them free by their own voluntary efforts."

The schools of New York were not free to all the children of the state until 1867. The super- intendent of that state speaks of its public-school system as "but an orderly plan of the people to educate themselves." At that time the city of Brooklyn had a course of study which was divided into six primary and six grammar grades, with a thirteenth grade added as an advanced course. Promotions were made semiannually after "careful examination of all the classes throughout the entire school at the same time."

Ohio reports the number of districts in which the teachers "boarded round" as 2025. The average number of pupils per teacher in the schools of Cincinnati at that time was 50.3 in the district school and 48.9 in the intermediate. In that city "the phonic method has now been very generally adopted in the schools as the basis for instruction in reading in the lower grades. Since the beginning of the year the department of drawing has been thoroughly reorganized. The superintendent of drawing gives regular lessons two days in the week and devotes the remainder of his time to supervision."

High schools are mentioned in the report from Pennsylvania:

Except in the matter of authorizing school directors to grade the schools where they can be graded, our school law makes no provision for the encouragement of higher education. A district may tax itself to establish and support a high school, but the state lends it no helping hand in doing so.

The city of Philadelphia reports that upwards of 20,000 children not attending any school are running the streets "in idleness and vagabondism. To enact a compulsory-education law without other essential provisions would be idle and chimerical. Not unless we clothe these 20,000 children and place them in point of appearance on a level with those who now occupy almost every seat, can our public schools open their doors for these outcasts of society and render them the same facilities afforded to the better class now in attendance."

We find the president of the Board of Education of that city offering this testimony as to the unorganized condition of the schools:

Had the public schools of Philadelphia the very necessary and competent services of a city superintendent to interpret, arrange, and execute our rules upon this and other kindred matters of school government and discipline, how readily could these conflicting views be harmonized and all difficulties and diversity of sentiment among the teachers adjusted. Let us hope that the time is not far distant when councils will see the imperative necessity of making appropriation necessary to secure the services of such an executive head for the public schools. Our duty is simply to legislate. We need a proper officer to execute the laws essential to the prosperity and unity of the system.

The fifty years since this was written have supplied many a superintendent to city boards of
education, but they have not disclosed many
boards of education with as clear a notion of
their duties as this board member had.

The references to the schools of Massachusetts in this report of the United States Commissioner of Education are particularly valuable,
for enough quotations from the school reports
of the towns are given to enable a reader to con-
struct a rather clear picture of the educational
situation in the mother commonwealth shortly
after the close of the war. The number of public
schools in the state for 1869 was 4959. The
average length of school was eight months and
four days, and 1085 male and 6937 female
teachers were employed. There were in the
state 175 high schools, 35 more than the law
required. There were also 45 incorporated
academies and 481 private schools and unin-
corporated academies, in which the amount paid
for tuition was estimated at $593,005, making
an aggregate of $3,716,892.40 expended in
the state in teaching its children. There are a

number of protests in the reports of the towns which tell in an incisive way what difficulties the schools were contending with. Among them are such statements as "One fourth of the time and money devoted to the schools is wasted and will be until parents manifest an increasing interest in the intellectual welfare of their children and consider it a duty to keep them regularly at school." "It is a remarkable fact that a majority of those who vote at town meeting against sufficient appropriations for a full term of free school are those who pay small taxes." "When our churches are magnificent and our houses are elegant, our temples of learning should not be barns." "To make a child think for himself is the teacher's main business. He should not aim to cram the memory of children with the results of his own thinking, but stimulate them to do their own thinking." "If the teacher would teach topics in such a way that each mind could grasp the thoughts, instead of requiring pupils to commit to memory only words, we should seldom be obliged to hear the too frequent remark, 'I have been over the

lessons but do not know anything about them.'" Education at the End of the Civil War
"Let the school hours and studies be few and pleasant, especially to the beginner, lest he learn to hate them before he knows their value and become a truant before he becomes a scholar." "The school in this town where most attention has been given to object instruction has done more work in the regular studies than any other of its grade." "There should be one school in town open to advanced scholars from all parts of the town for a term of twelve weeks at least. If so vast a majority of our children cannot go to the high school, it is important to take measures to bring some of the high-school studies to them."

In 1868 the town of Fall River established half-time schools "for children between the ages of 5 and 15 employed in the mills." One half of these children went to school in the forenoon and worked in the mill in the afternoon, the other half worked in the morning and went to school in the afternoon. Indian Orchard had a similar half-time school. It is clear from the ages included in this arrangement that child-labor laws are a creation of the last fifty years.

The city of Boston in 1870 reported that lessons in vocal and physical culture have been given in all the primary schools. Music is taught universally, and its study is considered of much importance. In some primary schools the phonic system of teaching reading has been employed and with success. There are thirteen special teachers of sewing.

In 1869 the district-school system was for a second time abolished, but its abolition was repealed the next year. It did not meet its doom in Massachusetts until the year 1882.

In short, our study shows that though in 1867 a beginning had been made in most of the activities of education, nothing more than a beginning had been made. The development, therefore, of all the great present-day agencies of education—free graded elementary schools, intermediate schools, high schools, normal schools, the great universities, schools for the negro and the Indian, vocational schools, the great foundations, departments in universities

for the study of education, statistical information concerning schools, new courses of study,
a vast literature about teaching, well-nigh the
whole present-day science of education (including school administration, child-study, educational psychology, the history and theory of
education, school hygiene, and educational
standards and measurements), and very nearly
the entire machinery of school supervision (city
superintendents, supervising principals, super-
visors of subjects, and state inspectors and
agents)—is a growth of the last fifty years. This
statement refers to changes so colossal that the
mere effort to think of them one after the other is
stupefying, but we have not begun to enumerate
them all. Our list makes no mention of school
buildings, play and playgrounds, compulsory
education, truant schools, juvenile courts, public
libraries, and a score more of agencies which
have been developed to assist the school in its
work. This whole accumulation of progress has
come about so gradually that it is only when we
set ourselves consciously to unravel its history
that we become aware how truly marvelous it is.

CHAPTER III

ET us examine its several parts a little
in detail. In 1871 New Jersey, the last
state in the United States to do so, abolished the rate bill, and the schools of the entire
nation became definitely free. In 1866, when
James A. Garfield made his report to the House
of Representatives urging it to establish a national
bureau of education, he referred to compulsory
school attendance in rather hesitating terms:

The genius of our government does not allow us
to establish a compulsory system of education, as is
done in some of the countries of Europe. There are
states in this Union, however, which have adopted a
compulsory system, and perhaps that is well. It is for
each state to determine. A distinguished gentleman
from Rhode Island told me lately that it is now the
law in that state that every child within its borders
shall attend school and that every vagrant child shall
be taken in charge by the authorities and sent to
school. It may be well for other states to pursue the
same course; but probably the general government
can do nothing of the sort.

43

The complaint is general in the first reports of the school authorities which the Commissioner of Education reproduces that children do not attend school; that parents are very remiss in their duty of sending them. Maine reports that "in general terms truancy and absenteeism deprive us of at least 25 per cent of attainable results in the educational line." Massachusetts was among the first to act, passing a compulsory-education law in 1852. Each town was authorized to establish "a reform school" for children between the ages of seven and sixteen who, "not attending school or without any regular occupation, are growing up in ignorance," and to send such children there instead of fining them, if it is thought best. Springfield reports that such a school was established in the almshouse, but, more significantly, that an ungraded school has also been established where habitual truants "who ought to be sent to the reform school may be kept under instruction until they can be returned to the graded schools." In 1870 the city of Boston employed ten truant officers who gave their entire time to investigating

44

cases of truancy and securing the attendance of absentees. It is a far cry from these beginnings to the more wholesome conditions of the pres- ent time. In 1916 all the states but one, Mississippi, and certain 'counties of Arkansas had compulsory-attendance laws; twenty-seven of them requiring attendance for the full school year and the others for a specified part of it, in no case less than twelve weeks. In 1870 the average number of years of schooling of two hundred days each received by each pupil in public and private schools was 3.36; in 1914 it was 6.16. The persistent effort to secure for all the children their right to an education which has characterized the last fifty years has produced a great number of agencies and devices for the protection of children, among them child-labor laws, which have been passed by most of the states and just recently by the nation (1916). In 1899 the state of Illinois created a juvenile court. The law which brought that wholesome child-saving agency into being has since been adopted by forty-four states and the District of Columbia. It has proved itself a real contribution to the world, for many foreign countries have adopted it. "I observe," says George Sorel in his "Reflections on Violence," "that nothing is more remarkable than the change which has taken place in the methods of bringing up children; formerly it was believed that the rod was the most necessary instrument of the schoolmaster; nowadays corporal punishments have disappeared from our public elementary schools." That statement is not literally true for the United States, but it is so nearly true that it may stand as perhaps the most significant proof which can be shown that civilization has really been in process of becoming in recent years. The modern school is a cheerful, happy place. In it teachers train rather than govern. Its first aim is to inculcate self-control. Flogging and a pallid quiet are no longer to be found in it. It is a workshop rather than a disciplinary cell. The suggestion which was made in the more optimistic years of its first decade that the twentieth century was to be the century of the child may not, let us hope, be so far wrong after all.

46

The course of study which the people of this *Some* democracy at the several periods of its history *Changes* have regarded as sufficient to prepare their chil- *since the* *CivilWar* dren for the work of life is a pretty good index of the real progress of the nation. The period of rigorous Puritanism from 1630 to 1750 brought up its children on the hornbook, the religious primer, the Psalter, the New and the Old Testament. In the period from 1750 to 1800 the spelling book took the place of the primer; in 1789 arithmetic was required by law in Massachusetts. Geography began to be "read" here and there about the year 1800. There was a bit of English grammar in the spelling books, and brief lessons were assigned in that subject at the beginning of the nineteenth century. "In some of the early editions [of the third part of my Institute published in 1785] I introduced short notices of the geography and history of the United States, and these led to more enlarged descriptions of the country," says Noah Webster. History was taught only in this incidental way until the second quarter of the nineteenth century.

47

There was imperative need for expansion of the course of study. The first address delivered before the American Institute of Instruction was upon the "Importance of Physical Education," by Dr. J. C. Warren. At its fourth meeting (1834) the Institute discussed the question "Can common schools be conducted profitably without the aid of bodily punishment?" and adopted a resolution "that the introduction of vocal music into our schools is an object of high importance to the community, and the American Institute of Instruction do hereby most cordially recommend it to public favor." A resolution of 1838 declared "it is desirable that the teaching of vocal music should be introduced into the common schools as soon as it may be practicable." A resolution was introduced in 1844 "that the time now devoted to the study of the dead languages as a part of collegiate education may be better employed upon other subjects," but was laid on the table.

In 1871 the Institute listened to an address on "Kindergartening the Gospel for Children," by Miss E. P. Peabody, but it was not until 1882 that it recommended "the teaching of draw- ing, not as an accomplishment but as a language for the graphic presentation of the facts and forms of objects."

The spirit of Pestalozzi brooded over the practice of education in the United States about the middle of the last century. Education, he said, is not memorizing the contents of books, it is learning to use one's own mind in doing something. It is growth from within outward, not from without inward. The dull bookwork of reading, writing, and ciphering was touched with life. The inclusion of object lessons introduced oral instruction, with all its beneficent, lively, free conversation about real things in place of the mumbling about abstractions which had previously comprised so large a part of school work.

The Schoolmaster of Yverdon transformed the schools of America as well as of Europe. "The importation of the Pestalozzian methods of the Home and Colonial School Society into the United States is the most striking development in American elementary education during

49

the middle of the nineteenth century," says Professor Parker. The first improvement was the
introduction of object lessons as an experiment
at the Oswego Normal School. Object teaching
soon became the leading subject for discussion
in teachers' institutes and spread widely in the
schools. In 1870 object lessons began to develop
into instruction in natural science as a system-
atic study for children in the elementary schools.
That in turn gave place to nature study in the
latter part of the nineteenth century, the dis-
tinction between them being that nature study
is the observational study of living objects and
processes for the sake of becoming familiar with
them, while the natural science which it dis-
placed was a highly technical endeavor to master
the general principles of science, which usually
resulted in only a verbal knowledge of them.

Geography was one of the sciences of the
Greeks. Its modern form is due to Humboldt
and Carl Ritter. Ritter, the scientist, about 1807
came under the influence of Pestalozzi, the
teacher, and undertook to prepare "a treatise
in his method on Geography." From that time

"the first step in a knowledge of geography is to know thoroughly the district where we live." This ideal teaching of geography as a study of man's relation to the earth, based on the personal investigation of every student who attempts to pursue it, is still fighting its way against mnemonic devotion to a text. Arnold Guyot, the pupil of Ritter, came from Switzerland to Massachusetts in the year 1848. For six years he was employed as an inspector and institute lecturer by the Massachusetts State Board of Education. In 1854 he was made professor of geology and physical geography at Princeton. Of his work he wrote:

During more than nine years it was my privilege to address thousands of teachers in the normal schools of Massachusetts and New Jersey, and in the teachers' institutes, on the subject of geographical teaching and the reform so much needed in that important department of instruction.

About the year 1866 he published a series of textbooks and also a manual on "Geographical Teaching." The task of carrying on the reform in geography teaching which Guyot had begun fell to Francis W. Parker. In season and out of season he preached its claims for a lifetime. He trained thousands of teachers, addressed hundreds of institutes, and in 1889 published his "How to teach Geography," "a practical exposition of methods and devices in teaching geography which apply the principles and plans of Ritter and Guyot" his editor calls it. But with these men the modern teaching of geography had only begun. Their work has been carried forward by scores of disciples and in every part of the land.

In 1821 Warren Colburn published his "First Lessons in Arithmetic on the Plan of Pestalozzi." The object of this book, as of Pestalozzi's teaching itself, was to banish ciphering as the mere carrying out of rules. Its whole purpose was to do away with ununderstandable abstractions by teaching little children in their very first lessons that all numbers are numbers of things. "The idea of number is first acquired by observing sensible objects," he said, and to prevent otherwise inevitable confusion no figures were introduced in the first fifty-five pages

of the book. Number ideas and number names
and mental operations with numbers were given
the complete right of way over figures, rules,
written work, and the ciphering of the past.
This plan commended itself to great numbers
of teachers, and the textbook which presented
it was very widely used. About the year 1870
an intensified Pestalozzianism, known as the
Grube method of teaching arithmetic, became
very popular in the United States. Each numeral,
according to this method, was treated by itself,
and the student learned to put it through all the
fundamental operations before he was allowed
to pass on to the next number. Such exhaustive
thoroughness was not only impossible to children but undesirable on the part of anyone, and
the rise of the Grube method was followed by
its fall in the early part of the period. But interest in the proper teaching of arithmetic has
grown with the years. The thinking arithmetic
which Warren Colburn struggled for has been
the aim not of all but of every informed teacher
who has come after him. Next to this the most
noteworthy change has been in a persistent effort

to modernize our rather archaic textbooks by omitting all subjects, methods, and problems which are not warranted by obvious applicability. A third change which has come about in arithmetic is the extended use of standardized tests to measure the work which children are able to do in it. We shall speak of these later.

The teaching of geography and arithmetic had begun to be rationalized here and there before the end of the Civil War. That work went forward. Object lessons had been introduced, and natural science and nature study followed them. New methods of teaching pupils to read began, as we have seen, to find favor. The worst method of teaching reading, the alphabet method, was practically the only method used from the earliest days of instruction in that subject by the Greeks down to our period. Comenius and the Jansenists found a better way, but their discovery did not change the universal A B C practice. The author of Worcester's "Primer," 1828, declared in his preface:

It is not, perhaps, very important that a child should know the letters before it begins to read. It

54

may learn first to read words, by seeing them, hearing them pronounced, and having their meanings illus- trated; and afterwards it may learn to analyze them or name the letters of which they are composed.

Horace Mann vigorously advocated the word method. But since the order of learning according to Pestalozzi was from simple to complex, there must be long drills, he said, upon the letters and after that long drills in forming letters into syllables and in making syllables into words. Consequently the influence of Pestalozzi and his followers upon the proper teaching of reading was harmful. It was not until the year 1870 that the A B C method began to be generally forsaken; so that the modern teaching of reading belongs almost entirely to the last fifty years. The Pestalozzian practice of reducing each subject to its lowest terms or elements and practicing at great length upon them and, finally, after this great mass of meaningless exercising had been performed, bringing the elements together into letters or words or sentences had as bad an effect upon the teaching of writing as it had upon the teaching of reading. The lessons which were given were not really lessons in writing. The letters were analyzed into strokes, — the straight, the outcurved, and the incurved. One must have drilled upon the strokes at very great length before he was considered fit to attempt to shape letters or to write words and sentences. Thus it will be seen that the educational bill of fare was pretty meager.

In 1869 several of the leading manufacturers of Massachusetts appealed to the legislature to direct the Board of Education to report "some definite plan for introducing schools for drawing or instruction in drawing free to all men, women, and children in all the towns of the commonwealth of more than 5000 inhabitants," saying "every branch of manufactures in which the citizens of Massachusetts are engaged requires in the details of the processes connected with it some knowledge of drawing and other arts of design on the part of the skilled workmen engaged." The Board of Education, being deeply impressed with the importance of the subject, intrusted its consideration to a special committee, which subsequently reported

that the almost total neglect of this branch of
learning in past times had been a great defect;
that we were behind many other nations in all
the means of art culture, a defect felt by native
artisans and mechanics, since "foreign workmen occupy the best and most responsible places
in our factories and workshops"; that agents
should be employed to go through the commonwealth and interest the people in this most
important subject; and that "teachers should be
required to be qualified to instruct in free-hand
drawing, and the work should be begun in the
primary departments and should be continued
with zeal and fidelity through the period of
school life." As a result, a law was passed in
1870 including drawing among the branches
of learning required to be taught in the public
schools and authorizing cities and towns of more
than 10,000 inhabitants to provide for free instruction in industrial or mechanical drawing to
persons over fifteen years of age, either in day or
evening schools. A supervisor of drawing was
imported from England in 1870, and in 1875
the Boston Normal Art School was established.

Manual training was introduced to the United States by an exhibit made by a Russian institution at the Centennial Exposition in Philadelphia in 1876. Schoolmen fought it bitterly for a time, but whereas in 1890 only 37 cities had made a place for it in their schools, by 1898 there were 146 cities in which it was taught.

The movement for school instruction in drawing, which had its beginning in Boston in 1870, was greatly stimulated by the Centennial Exposition of 1876. Nation-wide instruction in the fine and industrial arts, with all that marvelous development of taste and appreciation shown in more recent American manufactures and homes, is the result of that beginning.

In 1870 there were less than a dozen kindergartens in the United States, and all save one of them were conducted in the German language; the one English-speaking kindergarten had been opened in Boston in 1860 by Miss Elizabeth Peabody. Since that time the kindergarten has made its way into every corner of this land. In 1914 there were but 6 states whose laws did not provide for kindergartens, and in 1915

there were 9486 private and public kindergartens, with 10,877 teachers and 486,800
students in them. It is likely that by this time
not less than 4,000,000 children have profited
by its training, and perhaps as many as 30,000
young women have been instructed in the fine
art of providing opportunities for beginning
their education to young children, for whom
the beginning is still the most important part of
their entire course, even as it was to the discern-
ing mind of Plato. The introduction of the kindergarten into American education has been
called " the greatest step in the educational history of the country, with the exception of the
founding of normal schools." And perhaps the
most significant change which the kindergarten
has wrought, it has brought about indirectly,
through its wholesome modification of the
work which children do in the primary grades
and of the spirit in which they do it, rather than
directly through its own instruction.

For a comparative study of the changes
which have taken place in common schools,
that is, the public elementary and high schools

maintained by state and local taxation, we cannot do better than examine the following table from the report of the Commissioner of Education for the year 1916.

COMMON-SCHOOL STATISTICS OF THE UNITED

	1870	1875	1880	1885
Total population	[2] 38,558,371	[3] 43,700,554	[2] 50,155,783	[3] 56,221,868
Persons five to eighteen years of age	[2] 12,055,443	[3] 13,405,200	[2] 15,065,767	[3] 16,773,190
Pupils enrolled (duplicates excluded).	6,871,522	8,785,678	9,867,505	11,398,024
Per cent of total population enrolled	17.82	20.10	19.67	20.27
Per cent of persons five to eighteen years of age enrolled	57.00	65.54	65.50	67.96
Average daily attendance . .	4,077,347	5,248,114	6,144,143	7,297,529
Relation of same to enrollment (per cent)	59.3	59.7	62.3	64.0
Average length of school term (days)	[4] 132.2	130.4	130.3	130.7
Total number of days attended by all pupils	539,053,423	684,189,477	800,719,970	953,451,056
Average number of days attended by each person five to eighteen	44.7	51.0	53.1	56.8
Average number of days attended by each pupil enrolled	78.4	77.9	81.1	83.6
Male teachers	77,529	108,791	122,795	121,762
Female teachers	122,986	149,074	163,798	204,154
Whole number of teachers. .	200,515	257,865	286,593	325,916
Per cent of male teachers . .	38.7	42.2	42.8	37.4
Average monthly wages of male teachers [4]				
Average monthly wages of female teachers				
Average for all teachers [4] . .	$28.54	$32.55	$29.96	$34 22
Number of schoolhouses [5] . .	116,312	157,364	178,122	205,315
Value of all school property .	$130,383,008	$192,013,666	$209,571,718	$263,668,536

[1] The figures for this year are subject to correction.
[2] United States census.   [3] Estimated.

The number of persons from five to eight- *Some*
een years of age in the United States in 1914 *Changes*
was a little more than twice as many as in 1870, *since the*
but the number of pupils enrolled in school *Civil War*

STATES IN VARIOUS YEARS — GENERAL STATISTICS

1890	1895	1900	1905	1910	1914 [1]
[2] 62,622,250	[3] 68,844,341	[2] 75,602,515	[3] 82,584,061	[2] 91,972,266	98,781,324
[2] 18,543,201	[3] 19,911,050	[2] 21,404,322	[3] 23,410,800	[2] 24,239,948	26,002,153
12,722,581	14,243,765	15,503,110	16,468,300	17,813,852	19,153,786
20.32	20.69	20.51	19.94	19.56	19.39
68.61	71.54	72.43	70.35	73.49	73.66
8,153,635	9,548,722	10,632,772	11,481,531	12,827,307	14,216,459
64.1	67.0	68.6	69.7	72.1	74.2
134.7	139.5	144.3	150.9	157.5	158.7
1,098,232,725	1,331,775,201	1,534,822,633	1,732,845,238	2,011,477,065	2,255,657,142
59.2	66.9	71.8	74.0	83.0	86.7
86.3	93.5	99.0	105.2	113.0	117.8
125,525	129,706	126,588	110,532	110,481	114,662
238,397	268,336	296,474	349,737	412,729	465,396
363,922	398,042	423,062	460,269	523,210	580,058
34.5	32.6	29.9	24.0	21.1	19.8
	$46.82	$46.53	$55.04	$68.86	$79.94
	$39.41	$38.93	$42.69	$53.40	$62.57
$37.47	$41.02	$45.11	$51.10	$61.70	$66.07
224,526	239,630	248,279	256,826	265,474	276,460
$342,531,791	$440,666,022	$550,069,217	$733,446,805	$1,091,007,512	$1,444,666,859

[4] Several states are not included in this average.
[5] Including buildings rented.

COMMON–SCHOOL STATISTICS OF THE UNITED

	1870	1875	1880	1885
Receipts:				
From income of permanent funds and rents .				
From state taxes. . . .				
From local taxes. . . .				
From all other sources .				
Total received				
Per cent of total derived from —				
Income of permanent funds and rents				
State taxes				
Local taxes				
All other sources . . .				
Expenditures:				
For sites, buildings, furniture, libraries, and apparatus				
For salaries of superintendents and teachers .	$37,832.566	$54,722,250	$55,942,972	$72,878,993
For all other purposes . .				
Total expended . . .	$63,396,666	$83,504,007	$78,094,687	$110,328,375
Expenditure per capita of population	$1.64	$1.91	$1.56	$1.96
Expenditure per pupil in average attendance:				
For sites, buildings, etc. .				
For salaries	$9.28	$10.43	$9.10	$9.99
For all other purposes . .				
Total expenditure per pupil	$15.55	$15.91	$12.71	$15.12
Per cent of expenditure devoted to —				
Sites, buildings, etc. . .				
Salaries	59.7	65.5	71.6	66.1
All other purposes . . .				
Average expenditure per day for each pupil (cents)—				
For salaries	7.0	8.0	7.0	7.6
For all purposes	11.8	12.2	9.7	11.6

1890	1895	1900	1905	1910	1914 [1]
$7,744,765	$7,800,740	$9,152,274	$13,194,042	$14,096,555	$16,916,690
26,345,323	34,638,098	37,886,740	44,349,295	64,604,701	87,895,320
97,222,426	118,915,304	149,486,845	210,167,770	312,221,582	425,457,487
11,882,292	15,210,769	23,240,130	34,107,962	42,140,859	31,473,977
$143,194,806	$176,564,911	$219,765,989	$301,819,069	$433,063,697	$561,743,474
5.4	4.4	4.2	4.4	3.2	3.01
18.4	19.6	17.2	14.7	14.9	15.65
67.9	67.3	68.0	69.6	72.1	75.74
8.3	8.7	10.6	11.3	9.8	5.60
$26,207,041	$29,436,940	$35,450,820	$56,416,168	$69,978,370	$91,606,460
91,836,484	113,872,388	137,687,746	177,462,981	253,915,170	323,610,915
22,463,190	32,499,951	41,826,052	57,737,511	102,356,894	139,859,771
$140,506,715	$175,809,279	$214,964,618	$291,616,660	$426,250,434	$555,077,146
$2.24	$2.55	$2.84	$3.53	$4.64	$5.62
$3.21	$3.08	$3.33	$4.91	$5.46	$6.44
11.26	11.93	12.95	15.46	19.79	22.76
2.76	3.40	3.93	5.03	7.98	9.84
$17.23	$18.41	$20.21	$25.40	$33.23	$39.04
18.6	16.7	16.5	19.3	16.41	16.50
65.4	64.8	64.0	60.9	59.60	58.30
16.0	18.5	19.5	19.8	23.99	25.20
8.4	8.6	9.0	10.2	12.6	14.34
12.8	13.2	14.0	16.8	21.1	24.60

[1] The figures for this year are subject to correction.

was nearly three times as many in 1914 as in 1870, while the average daily attendance in 1914 was more than three times that of 1870. The average number of days attended by each person in 1870 was 44.7, in 1914 it was 86.7. The average monthly wages of teachers has increased from $28.54 to $66.07, while the number of schoolhouses has more than doubled, and the value of school property was more than eleven times as great in 1914 as in 1870. Moreover, the funds available for the maintenance of public schools were nearly four times as great in 1914 as they were but twenty-three years before, in 1892. Surely this is a record of which a country may well be proud.

But the table does not by any means tell the complete story of the changes which have taken place. The first graded schools came into being about 1860. Before that time primary schools were not generally regarded as a part of the school system, but were thought of as things apart and were very indifferently treated. They had to make their way into the system very much in the same way that the kindergartens

64

have since made theirs. The high schools also
were at first supplementary schools. They too
had to be integrated into the system. Supervision of instruction is almost wholly a thing of
the last fifty years. The first city superintendent
took office in Buffalo in 1837. Providence followed in 1839; New Orleans in 1841; Cleve-
land in 1844; Baltimore in 1849; Cincinnati
in 1850; Boston in 1851; New York, San
Francisco, and Jersey City in 1852; Newark
and Brooklyn in 1853; Chicago and St. Louis
in 1854; Philadelphia not until 1883. A school
system without a superintendent is practically
unthought of at the present time. At the beginning of this half century it was the rule and
its opposite the rare exception. It was in 1867
that William Torrey Harris became superintendent of schools of St. Louis, beginning thirteen
years of almost unequaled service as educator
of the American people. The course of study
which he made, the conceptions of education
which he championed,—as, for example, "Our
American idea rests on this principle: not what
the teacher does for the pupil, but what he gets

the pupil to do for himself is of value," " Every step toward the mastery of the printed page is a step toward freedom from and independence of living teachers. Thus our education is a giving of the conventionalities of a perpetual self-education,"— and the *Journal of Speculative Philosophy* which he edited (the first periodical devoted to philosophy anywhere published in the English tongue) demonstrate for all time what the office of city superintendent of schools at its best may be.

"The history of education since the time of Horace Mann," says Dr. Harris, "is very largely an account of the successive modifications introduced into elementary schools through the direct or indirect influence of the normal school." The 42 normal schools with which our period started had increased to 273 in 1914, 232 of them being public and 41 private schools. Besides, there were 1189 public and 292 private high schools offering training courses for teachers. In all a total of 131,998 students were being made acquainted with the functions of the teacher and habituated under direction to the work of teaching. The first normal schools re- ceived their pupils from the elementary schools. Framingham's requirements in 1867 were that the candidate must be at least sixteen years of age, must declare his intention to teach in the schools of Massachusetts, and "must present a certificate of good physical, intellectual, and moral character, and pass a satisfactory exami- nation in reading, spelling, writing, defining, grammar, geography, and arithmetic." "The course of study," says this same circular of 1867, "includes reading, with analysis of sounds and vocal gymnastics; writing; spelling, with deri- vations and definitions; punctuation; grammar, with analysis of the English language; arith- metic; algebra; geometry; physical and political geography, with map drawing; physiology; bot- any; zoölogy; natural philosophy; astronomy; mental and moral philosophy; school laws; theory and art of teaching; civil polity of Massa- chusetts and the United States; English liter- ature; vocal music; drawing. The Latin and French languages may be pursued as optional studies, but not to the neglect of the English

67

course." And all this was to be done in a two-year course! Dr. Harris declared at the semi-centennial celebration of the founding of the Framingham Normal School, in 1888, that "all normal-school work in the country follows substantially one tradition . . . and this traces back to the course laid down at Lexington in 1839." There have been great departures from that tradition since 1867. Normal schools now require their students to be graduates of high schools and find a two-year course all too short for proper instruction in the art of teaching. If we compare the training which they give now with the training of fifty years ago, their earlier efforts will be seen to be but a promise and beginning of the larger and more helpful work which they are doing to-day.

The first teachers' institute was assembled by Dr. Henry Barnard in Hartford, Connecticut, in 1839.[1] He regarded it as only a temporary device for giving teachers an "opportunity to revise and extend their knowledge of the studies

[1] Jacob S. Denman organized his first teachers' institute at Ithaca, on April 4, 1843.

usually pursued in district schools and of the best
methods of school arrangements, instruction,
and government under the recitations and lectures of experienced and well-known teachers
and educators." This "temporary device" has
lasted for seventy-seven years and has become a
permanent feature of the school life of every
state. The purpose of the institute has not
changed. The words of its founder still state its
program. In every corner of the land it provides
a means of educational rededication and professional renewing and bids fair to last in some
form or other as long as children and schools
and teachers exist.

The spread of these two agencies for the
training of teachers has during the last fifty
years been the distinctive thing about them.
While their work has been intensified, their
benefits have been made nearly universal. But
three new agencies for professional improvement have been created within that period.
One of them is the summer school, another the
Teachers' Reading Circle, and the third is university-extension courses. Chautauquas, after

the type of their original in New York State, have been held in many places. Summer schools have become almost a regular feature of normal-school, university, and college work. And university-extension teaching, after a period of lethargy, now seems to be firmly established both as a duty and a privilege of most of the great teaching centers. Certain states have thought it so indispensable that they have made it an integral part of their educational work. The Teachers' Reading Circle was the invention of an Ohio teacher in the year 1882. It is now a nearly nation-wide institution.

If we turn from elementary education, and the special agencies more particularly charged with conserving it, to secondary and higher education, we shall find the same phenomenal changes at work there also. The high school had but a fitful and uncertain status fifty years ago. In no department of education has such amazing development taken place in the last half century as in this. In 1826 Massachusetts directed every town of 500 households to employ a master to teach United States history,

bookkeeping, geometry, surveying, and algebra; and every town of 4000 inhabitants to
employ a master to teach Greek and Latin, history, rhetoric, and logic. It was the intention of
this law to universalize the high school within
the state. A law passed in 1848 brought it into
being here and there in Ohio. Legal permission
was given to organize higher grades in the public schools of Iowa in 1849, and county high
schools were authorized there in 1858. Boards of
education of union free school districts were authorized to establish academical departments in
1864 in New York State. Maryland legislated to
abolish academies and substitute high schools
for them in 1865. The high school seemed so
desirable and necessary that some communities
established it without waiting for authoriza-
tion of law. Efforts were made to prevent this.
In 1872 Judge Cooley's decision in the Kal-
amazoo case established the principle that "education not merely in the rudiments, but in an
enlarged sense was regarded as an important
practical advantage to be supplied at their
option to rich and poor alike." This greatly

71

encouraged the formation of high schools in
other states, as well as legalized them in Michigan. Wisconsin established a system of free high
schools in 1875 and Minnesota in 1881. Each
succeeding year has seen their number grow,
until in 1914 there was a total number of 11,515
public high schools, with 57,909 instructors
and 1,218,804 students. There were moreover
2199 private secondary schools, with 13,890
teachers and 154,857 students. No statistics
seem to be available to make possible a comparison of the number of schools in existence
at the beginning of the half century with the
number in existence at its close. Their tre-
mendous growth can, however, be indicated
by a comparison of the above figures with the
number of schools in existence in 1890, when
a total of 2526 public high schools, with 9120
teachers and 202,963 students, were reported.
There were at that time 1632 private schools,
with 7209 teachers and 94,931 students. That
is, there were more than three and one-third
times as many high schools, more than four and
one-third times as many teachers, and more

than four and one-third times as many students
in 1914 as there had been twenty-four years
before. The explanation of this remarkable
change is to be found in the more thorough
character of high-school instruction, in the
greater variety of courses which are offered,
and, above all, in a growing conviction on the
part of the American people that an elementary
education, no matter how good it may be, is
not sufficient preparation for the battle of life
on the part of the young. The time seems to be
rapidly approaching when public opinion will
demand some sort of high-school training for
all. At the beginning of our period the high
school was hardly a common school. Its chief,
and nearly its only function, was to teach Latin,
Greek, and mathematics to the small part of the
population which planned to go on to college.
That traditional task has colored all its work,
but is now the smallest part of it. It was solic-
itude "to give a child an education that shall
fit him for active life and shall serve as a foundation for eminence in his profession, whether
mercantile or mechanical," that led to the

73

founding of the first high school, in 1821. Though the high school was an outgrowth of the elementary school, the college practice of admitting students upon examination made it an adjunct to the college. At the beginning of the Civil War these examinations were in Latin, Greek, arithmetic, geography, English grammar, algebra, geometry, and ancient history. New subjects made their appearance in the college-entrance examinations in this order:

Modern history (United States), Michigan   1869
Physical geography, Michigan and Harvard   1870
English composition, Princeton   1870
Physical science, Harvard   1872
English literature, Harvard   1874
Modern language (foreign), Harvard   .   .   1875

Alternative courses and a large freedom of election began to be offered in colleges about the year 1869, and, as a consequence, courses other than the classical course began to be given in high schools. Their diversity has increased with the years, and now commercial courses, technical courses, manual-training and domestic-science courses, art courses, agricultural courses,

English scientific courses, etc., and frequently separate schools devoted to one or another of these forms of instruction, are much more in evidence than is the classical course of instruction from which they all sprang. The old method of passing from the high school to the college through the entrance way of examinations is still pretty completely in force in the eastern part of the United States. In the West an accrediting system, the outgrowth of that introduced by the University of Michigan in 1871, obtains. Innumerable conferences have been held for the purpose of improving the articulation between the high school and the college. That subject is temporarily in abeyance, for in more recent years the question of the relationship of the elementary school to the high school has supplanted it. The junior high school, or intermediate school, has been created to bridge the gap that formerly lay between them. That institution is as yet rather too new for statistical consideration. It took form in Berkeley, California, in the year 1908, and has been adopted in some form or other in many cities and towns of the United States. Fundamentally, it involves a reorganization of courses in the seventh and eighth grades of the elementary school, to provide for differentiation of work for pupils in accordance with their tastes, aptitudes, and probable future careers. This rearrangement of courses facilitates departmental teaching. In some places this reorganized upper-elementary school is combined with the first year of the high school, and a separate intermediate school is formed. This is the six, three, and three plan. Other redistributions are found. While the six, three, and three plan bids fair to be generally accepted, the period of preliminary experimentation is not yet over.

Another change to be noted is the lengthening of the high-school course by the addition of two years of college work. This is called the junior college. It too is still an experiment which as yet but few communities have been moved to try.

Vocational education, which is the oldest form of education of all, has asserted its claims with unusual vigor since the beginning of the twentieth century. After much agitation three types of schools have been evolved to prepare boys and girls over fourteen years of age for employment in agriculture and in the trades and industries: all-day schools, which aim to give opportunities for practicing a vocation on a productive basis; part-time schools, intended to give young workers an opportunity to extend their knowledge of their vocation or fit themselves for a new one; evening schools, to provide opportunity for mature workers to extend their knowledge of the vocations in which they are engaged during the day. Though this whole endeavor falls within this century, six or more states already have in operation definite plans for organizing and supervising vocational schools and assist local communities in financing them. These states are Massachusetts, New York, New Jersey, Pennsylvania, Wisconsin, and Indiana. At least four other states have made the beginnings of similar organization. Efforts to promote this type of education have already been so effective that the Smith-Hughes Bill has become a law, subsidizing vocational education in the several states by maximal grants of $7,000,000 per annum from the national treasury, this money to be given to the states for the salaries of vocational teachers and for the training of such teachers only upon condition that they expend an equal amount for the same purpose. With the development of vocational education the problem of vocational guidance has demanded attention and the beginnings of a helpful service to young people have been made.

Of the 563 colleges, universities, and technological schools in the United States in 1915, not less than 304 were established since the beginning of the year 1867. "The Illinois Industrial University," located at Champaign, Illinois, was founded in 1867, "to teach such branches of learning as are related to agriculture and the mechanic arts, not excluding other scientific and classical studies and military tactics." The preparatory department of the University of Minnesota was opened in 1867, and by 1869 a class had been fitted for the first college year. Cornell University was opened to students in 1868. The American college goes back to 1636 for its beginning, but the American university is almost entirely a creation of the last fifty years. The Yale catalogue of 1860–1861 contains the first announcement that the Ph.D. degree will be granted. Harvard did not announce it until 1872. It was not until 1890 that Harvard organized a separate graduate school. The University of Michigan offered the doctor's degree in philosophy in 1874. Johns Hopkins University was opened for instruction in 1876. It was primarily a graduate school from the first and has shaped university instruction throughout the entire country as perhaps no other influence has. The Massachusetts Institute of Technology was opened in 1865. Of the significant history and the vast influence of these and a score of other great teaching organizations the limits within which we work forbid us to speak; upon the teaching of medicine, law, and theology we may not enter, though changes as significant as any which we have mentioned have taken place in these great fields. For the education of atypical and defective children, as for each of these great subjects, a whole volume would be required.

Of the growth of scientific agriculture we must speak a little more at length. It began with the passage of the Morrill Act on July 2, 1862, in the midst of the Civil War. It increased so mightily that in 1914 there were 69 agricultural colleges, with 69,132 students and 6379 instructors. These places of agricultural learning have for some years been teaching from 60,000 to 80,000 students per year. Approximately 53 per cent of their graduates return to the farm, and 95 per cent devote themselves to agriculture in some form or other. Of those not graduating, practically all return to the land. In addition, very liberal provisions have been made by some of the states for the teaching of agriculture in the public schools. Massachusetts has developed a remarkable system of project work. New York State has recently adopted the township system of school control and has passed a law authorizing each town to employ a town director of agriculture, the state pledging itself to provide $600 as its contribution to his salary.

The higher education of women has been peculiarly a development of the last fifty years.

The Civil War left the work of teaching the young largely in the hands of women. They were so faithful in that which was committed to them that they were made rulers over more and more cities. If they were to teach, they must have opportunities for learning. When Michigan University opened its doors to them, in 1870, they were for the first time in the United States accorded equal opportunities with men in a thoroughly established college. All the state universities made provision for them. Of colleges for women, Vassar was opened in 1865, Wellesley in 1875, Smith in 1875, Bryn Mawr in 1885, Radcliffe in 1879, Barnard in 1889. All the universities save three or four are open to them. In 1870 but 30.7 per cent of the colleges were coeducational, and 69.3 per cent were for men only. In 1915, however, 70.7 per cent of the colleges open to men were coeducational, and 29.3 per cent for men only.

The education of the children of the negro race was one of the most serious problems that the nation confronted at the end of the war. The Freedmen's Bureau, created by Congress received no aid unless they were graded and had at least 100 pupils, with one teacher for every 50 pupils, and an average attendance of not less than 85 per cent. During the first four years of its existence this fund was used to assist the establishing of school systems in the cities of the South; for the next four years it was used to encourage the establishment of state school systems. In 1875 its secretary reported that all the states had established school systems and were maintaining them. The trustees of the fund thereupon devoted it to the proper training of teachers. They established a normal school at Nashville, and in order that it might leaven the entire South they created a large number of scholarships, of $200 each, to enable deserving students from all the Southern states to attend its classes. By 1903 this parent normal school was no longer needed, for it had secured the creation of state normal schools to foster the schools of each state. The trustees thereupon transformed the Peabody Normal School into the well-endowed Peabody College for the Training of Teachers.

In 1882 John F. Slater created a trust of $1,000,000 for the promotion of normal and industrial education among the children of freedmen. The income from this fund is used chiefly to pay the salaries of teachers of industrial pursuits in schools for colored students. A board of trustees was organized in 1908 to administer a fund of $1,000,000 given by Miss Anna T. Jeanes for fostering rural schools for negroes. This fund is used in several ways: in some districts county superintendents are assigned a superior teacher of industrial work, whose duty it is to introduce such work into the rural schools of the county and to supervise it; in other districts a teacher is assigned to a central school and does extension work in the schools of the region about it; a third method consists in coöperating with local communities in lengthening the school term. Another fund of $1,000,000, the Phelps-Stokes fund, assists by making researches, endowing scholarships, etc. The General Education Board, incorporated in 1903 for "the promotion of education within the United States of America without distinction of race, sex, or

creed," and which controls a fund of some $46,000,000, originally devoted its resources to the promotion of secondary, rural, and negro education in the Southern states. Since 1905 it has taken the entire country for its province, and more recently it has planned to assist medical education in China. It is chiefly concerned with the promotion of agriculture in the South, the development of a system of secondary schools there, and the promotion of higher education throughout the nation. With such encouragement as these great organizations have been able to give the education of the colored race, it is clear that progress altogether unprecedented in the history of the world has been made. The average of life has risen so rapidly, and colored men who were born in slavery have attained such usefulness and leadership in the short period since the war, as to encourage a confident hopefulness for the future of their race. The work of Booker T. Washington alone has transformed the status of a people. It is a significant fact that the industrial training developed in the colored schools has blazed a

86

path which education is to-day taking throughout the nation.

In addition to those already mentioned, three other great endowments have been made for the promotion of education. One of these is the Carnegie Institution at Washington. It took form in 1907 and is a corporation "to encourage in the broadest and most liberal manner investigation, research, and discovery, and the application of knowledge to the improvement of mankind." It has a fund of $22,000,000 for that purpose.

In the year 1906 Mr. Carnegie created a Foundation for the Advancement of Teaching, endowing it with $10,000,000, to which sum in 1908 he added $5,000,000. "I have reached the conclusion," said Mr. Carnegie, "that the least rewarded of all the professions is that of the teacher in our higher educational institutions. . . . I have transferred to you, and to your successors as trustees, $10,000,000, the revenue from which is to provide retiring pensions for the teachers of universities, colleges, and technical schools in our country, Canada, and

Newfoundland, under such conditions as you may adopt from time to time."

The Russell Sage Foundation was created in 1907, by a gift of $10,000,000 from Mrs. Sage, for the "improvement of social and living conditions in the United States of America." Its trustees decided at the beginning that its primary function is "to eradicate as far as possible the causes of poverty and ignorance rather than to relieve the sufferings of those who are poor or ignorant." Among its activities has been a persistent study of the ways of measuring educational progress and results, and a series of important investigations of the problem of retardation and elimination in the public schools. Very important school surveys have been made by its educational staff. The total bequests to education from 1871 to 1914, inclusive, is reported by the United States Commissioner of Education as $584,418,082.

It is fitting since we began with science that we should end with science. There is no magic about it, nothing but the patience to answer human problems by examining minutely facts

88

which bear upon them. This same minuter ex- Some
amining of facts which in fifty years produced Changes
a new medicine has produced a new education. since the
Three hundred years ago Richard Mulcaster Civil War
urged the importance of a serious study of education. "I conclude," he said, "that this trade
requireth a particular college for these four
causes. First, for the subject, being the means
to make or mar the whole fry of our state. Sec-
ondly, for the number, whether of them that
are to learn or of them that are to teach. Thirdly,
for the necessity of the profession, which may
not be spared. Fourthly, for the matter of their
study, which is comparable to the greatest pos-
sessions, for language, for judgment, for skill
how to train, for variety in all points of learning, wherein the framing of the mind and the
exercising of the body craveth exquisite consideration, besides the staidness of the person."
College authorities were deaf to this proposal
and blind to this need until President Wayland
sought to establish a course of instruction in the
science of teaching at Brown University in 1850.
His efforts were not successful. Horace Mann

introduced such a course as an elective study at
Antioch College in 1853. The University of
Iowa had a normal department from 1856 to
1873, which became a chair of didactics after
that date. In 1874 President Angell recommended that lectures be given to the senior class
of the University of Michigan on the organizing and management of schools and the art of
teaching. In 1879 the Regents, on the recommendation of the president and faculty of that
university, established a chair of science and
art of teaching, with the fivefold purpose, as
they declared, of fitting university students for
the higher positions in the public-school service, of promoting the science of education, of
teaching the history and theory of education,
of securing to teaching the rights and preroga-
tives of a profession, and of giving a more per-
fect unity to the state educational system.

Since that time many universities and colleges have created similar chairs, which have
not been slow in becoming energetic departments. For a long time their occupants were
regarded with a good deal of suspicion by their

more conservative colleagues in the academic family. They were not slow, however, in proving their usefulness, and it soon became apparent that the interest which they represented was too serious and far-reaching to be conserved by such inadequate means.

Clark University, which opened in 1889, made ampler provision for it; and in 1898 Teachers College became a professional school of Columbia University, taking rank with the schools of law, medicine, and applied science. The University of Chicago has also established a college of education, and schools of education are now to be found in nearly all of the larger universities.

This institutional study of education is a twentieth-century activity. Its first fruits are a clearer comprehension of educational principles and a more thorough organization of educational machinery. Energetic research has already been as profitable in this field as in other fields of science.

One of our most capable historians of education values what has been achieved in this direction so highly that he does not hesitate to say that John Dewey's discovery that real education is and must be based upon the nature of the child and E. L. Thorndike's discovery of a method of scientifically measuring educational results will in time be ranked in importance with Darwin's conception of evolution. Rousseau's adjuration "Study your pupil, for it is evident that you know nothing about him" has been a controlling principle in the last four decades. A science of child psychology came into being, and psychological conceptions and methods took the place of empirical notions and rule-of-thumb devices of an earlier time. Herbart's reconstructions of educational doctrine contributed to this movement. Physiology and psychology taught the schoolmaster that the human organism is an action system. Passivity in learning was abandoned, and methods of training through activity were substituted for it. The newly discovered science of medicine and the new education joined forces to conserve the physical well-being of the growing child. Activistic psychology revealed the importance of

Nature's method of training him by play. Scientific study of administration and of methods of
instruction led to a reorganization of schools,
and school surveying came into being as a
method of determining whether or not conditions called for improvement and of deciding
what that improvement should be. The effort to
evaluate instruction necessitated the formula-
tion of standards and measuring scales with
which to detect the presence or absence of the
results required. That particular endeavor is still
in its earlier stages, but bureaus for measuring
and testing the sufficiency of the processes and
the products of instruction have been created in
several places. The study of sociology has contributed substantially to the remaking of educational theory. The pragmatic philosophy, with
its revolutionary conception of the nature and
function of knowledge, has just begun to revise
educational aims and remake programs of study.
Newer and truer educational rallying cries begin
to sound above the call to get knowledge for
the sake of knowledge and science for the sake
of science. Purposive education begins to banish

93

aimless learning from the field. The doctrine of formal or general discipline, which directed the pursuit of certain studies for the development of the faculties or powers of the mind, has been scientifically tested and found wanting. A philosophy of education can no longer be made out of it. When it is given up, as it must be, only specific education will remain, but specific education so rich in variety and so definite in purpose and method that it promises results far better than those which the old training gave.

Thus at the end of fifty years of unparalleled progress the world waits impatiently for the coming of peace to begin a yet greater cycle of educational renewing.

A BRIEF BIBLIOGRAPHY

BOONE, RICHARD J. Education in the United States. D. Appleton and Company, New York.

BROWN, ELMER E. The Making of our Middle Schools. Longmans, Green, & Co., New York.

BUTLER, NICHOLAS MURRAY (Editor). Monographs on Education. Department of Education for the United States Commission to the Paris Exposition of 1900.

CARLTON, FRANK. "Economic Influences upon Educational Advance in the United States, 1820–1850," Bulletin of the University of Wisconsin, 1908.

CUBBERLY, E. P. Changing Conceptions of Education. Houghton Mifflin Company, Boston.

FINEGAN, THOMAS E. Teacher Training Agencies. Eleventh Annual Report of the State Department of Education, Vol. II, Albany, New York.

HANAFORD, PHEBE A. The Life of George Peabody. B. B. Russell, Boston.

MANN, MRS. MARY (Editor). Life and Works of Horace Mann. Horace B. Fuller, Boston.

MARTIN, GEORGE H. The Evolution of the Massachusetts Public School System. D. Appleton and Company, New York.

PARKER, S. C.   A History of Modern Elementary Education. Ginn and Company, Boston.

THWING, CHARLES F.   A History of Higher Education in America. D. Appleton and Company, New York.

Proceedings of the American Institute of Instruction.

The Reports of the Massachusetts Board of Education.

Reports of the School Committee of Boston.

The Reports of the United States Commissioner of Education (particularly the earlier ones).